THE GOD OF SAN FRANCISCO

Sibling Rivalry Press, LLC
PO Box 26147
Little Rock, AR 72221

info@siblingrivalrypress.com

www.siblingrivalrypress.com

ISBN: 978-1-943977-81-9
Library of Congress Control Number: 2020939505

By special invitation, this title is housed in the Rare Book and Special Collections Vault of the Library of Congress.

First Sibling Rivalry Press Edition, November 2020

THE GOD OF

POEMS BY

JAMES J.
SIEGEL

SIBLING RIVALRY PRESS
DISTURB/ENRAPTURE
LITTLE ROCK, ARKANSAS

CONTENTS

FOR DESI

DECEMBER 1

The Sisters are lighting candles
on the corner of 18th and Castro.
Kabuki-faced, corseted,
these are not the nuns who haunted
the hallways of my Catholic adolescence.
These nuns have names like
Sister Anni Coque L'doo
and Sister Porn Again.

Eyelashes longer than their patent leather heels
they are towering Magdalenes
casting angelic shadows
over little hunchbacked ladies.
Wire-rimmed glasses, beauty shop hair,
red ribbons pinned to lapels,
they clutch family photos and recite
the names of the dead like novenas
while the evening traffic idles in the intersection.

I wait at the signal and listen
to the lamentation of lost brothers,
sons that never came home.
Below my feet the sidewalk shakes,
gently shifts,
as I realize this is the epicenter,
the place where death devoured
one brilliant light after another.

This is where life ended
but went on for those left behind,
for those who called the mortuary,
bought the flowers, wrote the obituary,
chose the headstone or urn,
cleaned out the closets,
gave away shirts and shoes,
opened windows to let in the sun,

changed the sheets,
woke each morning and decided
to keep going on.

The San Francisco sun makes way
for the great procession of fog
and the flames are dancing on their wicks.
Soon the boys will come out of hiding,
slumbering off their morning hangovers
to start it all over again.

I hear a rosary clicking
and the ticking of seconds at the crosswalk.
I hear a boozy cry escape a neighborhood bar
and I remember that my friends are waiting
for me to buy the next round.
So I cross the street,
pass this great iconography.
I walk by and never look back
because I am still young
and foolish,
and believe I will live forever.

GAY CANCER

When men died of gay cancer
I was only five—preoccupied
combing the manes of
purple ponies,
bending Barbie's legs to fit
snug in her pink convertible.

The nightly news was a montage
of pale skin and pitted cheeks—
thin, thin bodies and fevered eyes.
Then back to regular programming—
sequined Solid Gold Dancers
twirling to the week's top ten.

I twirled in my driveway like
Lynda Carter in her star-spangled shorts
while the white-hot sun bleached
the neighborhood streets
and the GRID sparked to life.

That was the summer a sick boy
took a dip in the city pool.
So they drained the water,
scrubbed the tiles clean
and waited for the all-clear.
No one could be too safe.

So we made due with the Slip 'N Slide,
grape Kool-Aid and Rocket Pops,
our mothers with their menthols,
lawn chairs and lemonade,
deconstructing the perfect Hollywood male—
Tom Selleck versus Burt Reynolds.

And sometimes they whispered
theories on transmission—saliva, blood,

soft men—loose-hipped and high-heeled
wasting away in San Francisco, New York,
one or two in Toledo, Ohio,
if the gossip was true.

I left adult talk to adults
and helped by best friend wrap
her hair in Princess Leia buns,
ignored the debates on disease, disappointment,
a boy's unnatural desire to slip
his bare foot in a sheer stocking.

The years that followed brought us
the great nail polish panic,
licorice-red fingers and toes,
Ryan White in Kokomo,
bullets shot through his living room window.
We could never be too safe.

So my mother locked up her makeup case
and my father pulled me under
the remains of a rusted Chevy Blazer,
pointing out car parts like constellations,
slowly, patiently teaching me
the importance of fixing damaged pieces.

SUNDAY EVENINGS IN THE ERA OF REAGAN

I ride with my father in a rusted Chevy Blazer—
windows open, smell of gasoline,
summer storm on the air.
It is garbage night.
Fireflies flickering.
Radio turned to Yankees baseball.

My father has his routine.
Starting at the end of the neighborhood,
then taking side street after side street
until we arrive back home. He knows
every house and address where the owners
throw out what can be recycled—
ten-cent aluminum cans,
stacks of newspaper tied with twine.

The car idles and New York hits a line drive.
My father hops out,
surveys the scene of trashcans
before snagging a bag of bottles.
He tosses them in the backseat
and we are on the move again,
the first drops speckling the windshield.

When the next house is on the passenger side
my father points out which bags to grab.
I am hesitant.   I am humiliated.
The car door creaks and moans
and I know I will be seen,
shadow of a boy captured
in a porchlight glow,
the soles of his Converse coming unglued,
rummaging through refuse,
someone else's junk and debris.

Back in the safety of the car I am a selfish thing,

arms folded around me, sinking in my seat
as a crowd in the Bronx erupts in cheers,
tears of anger sticking in my eyes.
   I do not yet understand
this decade of layoffs and scab wages,
union busting and the trickle-down
that never came. I do not understand
sacrificing to keep the lights on,
the little extra that will pay tuition,
next year's school uniforms.
I do not understand my father
doing the best he can do.

The next morning I wake to crunching metal.
My father is in the garage
crushing cans with a sledgehammer.
He goes row by row,
assembly line precision
flattening each can to a tin disk.
He lets me try my hand, but I am clumsy,
unsteady.

Soon we are filling plastic bags with flattened cans
bound for the recycling center
where we dump our collection on conveyor belts,
separating paper from plastic. It is a thrill
to watch the things we found sailing away,
the machines growling and grinding,
chewing up glass.

My father cashes in his receipts,
counts out one-dollar bills.
Placing them in my hand he says,
   For the help.
He says I can do whatever I want,
save it or play arcade games,
buy a comic book or two.
I can do with it whatever I choose.

CRABAPPLES

In the grey November light
I play in the backyard where
the crabapple tree meets the property line—
limbs bare for all the neighbors to see.

       I am alone—as I am always alone—
because I never learned to throw a ball
or tell lies to a teacher. I am a strange
character in the games I create—
sometimes a knight, other times sorceress.
But always a twig in hand
as a sword or magical staff—
brandishing a dangerous duality.

The gnarled tree roots are the cloven feet
of a minotaur. The fenced yard a labyrinth
where I change the corridor walls to my will,
always running through the fantasies in my head.

On other days that tree is a towering crone,
her bulbous fingers pointing to the silent skies—
the impending darkness, moon on the rise.
And the ground is a field of fiery bombs,
the eyes of hellcats burning in the brown grass.
They harden in the autumn
purring out a premonition—
the jays and robins are on their way
to pluck away the dying fruit.

The wind blows in and the branches
creak and cackle. The first clouds
tumble in with rain.
And in the distance the church
clangs its mechanical bells.
A siren song. Tornado signal.
There is nowhere to run.

No way to hold off the outside
world crashing in. It is an elegy,
a dirge for the safe days
hiding away.

AUTUMN BURNING

Driving 75
I see a blackened sky
like the underworld is set to rise—
it's a sky I've seen before
when autumn begins to die.

Last season's debris
dragged onto the pile—
a tower of rubber tires,
railroad ties,
the dead and rusted pines.

It's a monument
of barn doors and porch swings,
a witch's pyre
waiting for hellfire,
the snap of a match,
a spark that swells to a blaze.

Soon the wind spurs
an ember to an inferno,
turns a farmer's field
to lakes of flames.
Soon the cloudless day
is dark ash—
a claw of smoldering carbons
reaching out to grasp
the early evening moon.

Through the car window
I can taste the dawn of winter,
scorched wood, melting plastic,
diesel fumes and fresh-cut grass.

From the highway overpass
I see the earth as Hades,

the Gehenna of Ohio,
flatlands turned to something fearful—
end of days,
frolicking demons
tossing souls to the abyss.

I would look away in terror,
take a different exit,
if it were not so beautiful—
all the things we no longer need
offered as a fiery atonement,
consumed by a brilliant holocaust.

WYOMING

By the time we reach Wyoming
there is nothing but snow. Eighteen-wheelers
throttle along leaving trails of serpentine mist.

West of Laramie there is no choice
but to take the next exit,
find the first vacancy. Cowering
in the icy drifts we discover
a tin-roofed motel—a relic
of some grey ghost town day.
And we discover we are frightened
of the locals seeing us together.
So my husband stays behind
in the warmth of the running car
as I ring the bell that wakes the owner
from a heavy hibernation.

Thread-bare robe, white hair standing on end,
a bespectacled old man gives me the once-over.
Little is said—but his hardened face speaks
to a suspicion for strangers,
a disdain for the new world
creeping in or passing through,
a world permanently changed
since a tortured body was found on the plains.
His office walls are a forest of antlered animals,
deer and elk staring into a lost distance
as though death has come along
without warning.

Soon I am hiding with my husband
in a room that does not keep out the cold,
does not keep us safe from wondering
who is sleeping on the other side
of thin walls aged with tobacco smoke.
In our down-wool coats

we cling to one another
because the heater is broken,
because we are not yet in San Francisco,
and the night is a blizzard of noise.
A lodger snores. A TV drones.
And something screams out in the darkness—
the wind racing down the highway,
a hunted animal desperate for shelter.

TWENTY-NINE DAYS OF RAIN

At first I found the humor in it—
the flooded streets, the rushing waters,
trash cans yanked from the sidewalk
to sail away like untethered canoes. Broken
umbrellas—inside out, spines cracked,
as though they took one last gasp, pleading
with their owners,   *Go on without me.*

For a week or so I even found the beauty—
lovers pulling one coat over their heads,
skipping puddles to catch a cab.
The miniature Mississippi River
running the length of the restaurant window,
two friends at a table sharing a bottle of wine,
their blurry reflection like two swimmers
dining at the bottom of a lake.

But now I'm tired of beauty
and laughter. Tired of wet socks and pant legs,
the dirty pavement crack ponds I always step in.
Sleepless from the night clouds galloping past
the rooftops, sparks of lightning from their hooves.
Tired of the churning worry in the gut
that tells me San Francisco was a mistake.

The weight of water on the lungs,
the heft of an ocean on the heart,
to admit that mistake. Crossing the continent—
two thousand miles in three days,
a West Coast plan and everything
I own stuffed in the trunk of the car.
And all those I love left behind
only to say,   *I was wrong.*

I need these inkwell skies to dry,
for that California light to bend

through the bedroom window
and shake me awake. I need to fall
in love again with the curves of Lombard Street,
sunset flickering on the waves of the bay,
the bright possibility of calling this place home.

I need a cable car postcard day—
tourists cresting the Powell Street hill,
the Saint Francis Hotel and Union Square,
seagulls circling a perfect blue sky. I need
to put a stamp on this, mail it back to Ohio,
a short note scrawled on the side,
San Francisco is beautiful, and I am doing just fine.

ELEGY FOR THE CASTRO FUNERAL HOME

One hundred years and you are gone.
Death is not the business it once was.
Monument to loss—your crumbling
façade a reminder of days we would rather
forget.   But forgetting
is just more dying.

          So who will remember you
when the bulldozer and the wrecking
ball levels your walls, clears the way
for more overpriced homes?

When new bones rise from your foundation
and jackhammers turn concrete to dust
will anyone listen for benedictions
haunting the dusty air?
Will anyone pry loose a century of eulogies
trapped in the earth? And will they pour forth
from the pavement cracks like steam—
a pale ghost—ascending the sky?

From your ashes a tower of condos
for the living—East Coast dreamers seeking
a California mythology, too young to know
the power of death or a quilt of names a mile long.
Will they know where they sleep at night?
And will they wake in dark hours to the sweet
perfume of gardenias, lilies? Wake to the burning
of vigil candles, the honey scent of soft wax,
smoke and ember from dying flames?

And when they gut your front parlor
for a coffee shop or sidewalk café,
will anyone remember the dead in repose?
Will anyone sip a morning brew and witness
phantom pallbearers, another casket carried

out your front door? Day after day,
week after week—how did you keep up
with death's punctual schedule?
As many as three funerals a day
in that decade of decimation.

Will anyone remember you
as the only mortuary in San Francisco
to open its doors to the victims of AIDS?
In those days even the dead were turned away.
But you dressed them in suits and ties,
washed and combed their hair, powdered
the skin to hide the scars and sores,
made them into handsome young men again.

So will we remember or will we build
and build again? Turning earth over and
over until history is another buried thing.

THEY STILL SAY FAGGOT IN SAN FRANCISCO

It is a word I still hear
when the MUNI train pulls into Castro station—
Faggot.   As in
      This is where the faggots get off or
      This is where all the faggots live.
It is just a word
from the Old French, Middle English—
fagot—literally meaning
a bundle of sticks,
branches bound together for a torch,
a binding.

It is only a word
and still I flinch as though I bit my tongue.
I cringe because this is San Francisco,
city in a catsuit purring at the moon,
leather pups pawing their masters at Folsom.
This is not Wyoming, rural Ohio.
This is not my Catholic school or a Bible Belt country club.
This is where rainbow flags umbrella the sky
like a queer force field, a kaleidoscope bubble of
security.   And still

I look over my shoulder when walking home alone
because a queen was beaten leaving the Eagle. Not a mugging.
Nothing taken. The only desire was to blacken the eyes, break a tooth,
stain the concrete with faggot blood.

Fagot—a noun derived from the verb—faggoting,
the forging of steel and iron rods. It reminds me
of 9-irons in the back of a pickup truck, the young men
who drive into San Francisco on Pride weekend,
hunting queers leaving the parades, waiting
to blare their horns, flash their headlights, scream
faggot.

Faygeleh—an old Yiddish word—meaning little bird,
makes me think of Feather Lynn, a Radical Faerie
beaten until unconscious. A Sunday morning,
left to die on the street where Church meets Duboce.
Fragile body. Broken wings. And yet I know
that spirit is rising.

Faggot—dating back to the 16th Century—as in
the faggot and the stake, the burning of heretics.
A word even I use when I find the ones I love,
when I find my friends at the bar,
 Good evening my beautiful faggots,
 this first drink is on me
because we are still a dying breed
and I am a pillar of fire. I am
an extraordinary conflagration.
A beautiful immolation.
I am flaming.

DARK ARTS

Satan takes his brush
dipped from the darkest palette,
          and paints through the night.

He spills out the world
like stars scattered on the sky,
          nova exploding.

A lover of form
he marvels at the masters,
          their shadows and light.

Francisco Goya—
Saturn Devouring His Son—
          swells his crackling heart.

Fuseli's *Nightmare*—
incubus perched on the chest—
          a beautiful dream.

The millennia
trample by on wild horses
          dragging dead witches.

And he finds his muse
in portraits of cruelty,
          the devil's still life—

flowers in a vase,
universe of black blossoms
          bursting into life.

His new age begins
in bright, vivid hues of pain
          on canvases of flesh—

scarlet monochrome
on genocide's tapestry
spilling native blood.

Grey engines of smoke
and train cars of yellow stars
framed in gypsy bone.

Iconography
of false prophets, messiahs,
pigments of Jonestown.

And warm orange flames
of hellfire, the black churches
blazing in Dixie.

His inspiration,
his great grotesque renaissance,
carries on and on.

He is no artist,
but docent to humankind
choking on freewill.

Works of human art,
accomplished without devils
or incantation.

Just the divine soul—
God's flawed expert creation—
doing what it knows.

SISTER ROSE

My Aunt Rose was buried in her habit,
a Carmelite nun since she was a teen.
For sixty years the bell called her to prayer,
the morning prayer of praise, the white mantle
worn to receive the great body of Christ.
The midday hours filled with manual work—
sewing machine purring in the cloister,
the gardens weeded, the vegetables canned.
At recreation rosaries were made,
then again more prayer, singing in the choir,
back to labor and sweeping the stone stairs.
Vespers, a meager meal, twilight matins
before the nuns retire to their cells,
a weary body offered to the Lord.
Sweet Jesus on her lips she shut her eyes
one last time. Casket of satin and brass
closed on a simple life of devotion,
buried in a Catholic cemetery,
a vast garden of sandstone disciples,
marble pietas and weeping Marys.

As a child I believed this was heaven,
a never-ending sea of mausoleums,
a Vatican City of monuments,
and tiny nuns hurrying to their posts,
their earthly duties continuing on—
polishing the pearly gates to sparkle,
darning the flowing togas of angels.
Every day a Sunday benediction,
a cold cathedral, a wooden kneeler,
a sky filled with rumbling organ thunder.
Father, Son, and Holy Ghost looking down,
but dim and distant as December light,
unreachable as the earthly word.
I would listen to those funeral bells

echoing from here to the hereafter,
watch the setting sun stretch out the shadows
of iron gates, looming crucifixes,
and promise myself I would never die.

BILINGUAL

This is larger than the lightning
simmering over the Sierra Madre.
Let's cool this down a bit,
all this rolling around on beds
and beaches and the business
of joining lives together.

It's been a long time
since I held two languages on my tongue.
It is not as simple as sharing the salt off a glass,
letting it shine on your lips
and laughing as though life were effortless.

It is not as easy as falling in love
with the rain-slick cobblestones,
the way the skin sticks to the leather
in the backseat of the cab,
your hand on top of mine.

There is little romance
in conjugating verbs,
managing the masculine and feminine,
remembering the proper pronunciation
of another's wants and needs.

Sometimes I make as much sense as a Latin mass
or a night of heavy drinking.
And you may need to interpret
what is real and what is my madness,
whether it is a full moon
or just one of my moods.

There is nothing I want more
than the hot heat of the moment,
to melt in the embrace of the Mexican sun,

but these things do not last.
These things come like high seasons
and what remains is the vernacular,
the continual awareness of our voices.

TEOTIHUACÁN

Chocolate chihuahua—
only four pounds and a few small ounces.
We named you with great honor,
your motherland,
the metropolis of Teotihuacán—
for short we call you Teo.

Birthplace of the sun and moon
where the gods built their pyramids,
your ancestors were something close to deities.
The bones of your brothers
found with the bones of children.
In the afterlife you would need to lead
the tribes of Mexico across the great seas
separating Earth from the other side.

But you have never been fond of water,
your hindquarters shivering in the bath,
your sad eyes in the soapy sink.
And on rainy days you run and hide,
refusing the leash, the long walk,
you would rather pee inside the house.

And you have no love for children.
Their unpredictable movements,
their grabby hands unnerve you.
When they howl with pleasure
it pierces your delicate ears.
When they totter in your direction
your face contorts to something mythological,
the snarl of the chupacabra,
the vampire bat draining blood from a cow.

And forget rising from the dead.
Your sunny days are wasted
safely tucked away in your bed.
There are balls and Frisbees to catch

but you would rather chase rabbits in your dreams.
Your blankets rise and fall
with the rhythm of your snores.
You only come alive with a bribe—
the whir of a can opener,
fresh kibble clinking into your bowl.

So it is difficult
to picture your face on Mayan pottery,
your image painted on a cave mural.
But then I find you,
nose to the carpet, tail to the sky,
on the trail of something left behind.
I find you digging the depths of the couch cushions,
pawing with precision until you discover
the remains of last night's popcorn,
a fossilized potato chip.
Your eyes beam with pride
as you lick crumbs from your whiskers.
And I am a believer
that even you could sniff out the underworld.

FALLING ASLEEP TO THE SOUND
OF FOG HORNS I DREAM OF OHIO

Night pulls down a curtain of fog,
tucking away the Golden Gate. Soon
the horns are bellowing their low, throaty moan.

It is late.
I am tired and wavering between sleep and the ocean's cries,
but I cannot stop myself from traveling over time zones,
to places I've lost.

Three hours ahead the Jeep plant releases its graveyard shift.
Men spill out from metal doors, empty thermoses in hand.
The morning light struggles to reach the horizon.
Chain-link gates drag back, ushering out a procession of American cars.

I wonder where they go
when the work whistle halts the assembly line.
Perhaps the Captain's Quarters for a rum and Coke,
a double for the double shift.
The bar stool is an old friend
and the bartender has a tender face—
gin-blossomed and aged but friendly.
He knows everyone by name,
by their factory-chapped hands,
and the first drink is always on the house.
There is peace
in a sweaty rock glass,
the sun throwing golden lassos over liquor bottles,
the linoleum floor,
ancient remains of ashtrays.

But then I remember the Captain's Quarters is gone
like everything else that is gone.

So perhaps the night ends
with the drapes drawn on a living room,

its dog-bitten couch,
flea market quilt,
the ache of sixteen hours on foot,
the clang of machinery still ringing in the ear.
Perhaps those men fade away
to a locomotive drone,
the chugging of boxcars lurching out of Toledo
for the great train yards of Chicago.
Those miles are a mystery
like waking but dreaming of faraway places—
California,
San Francisco,
a weightless city settling on a fog.
It is nothing like Ohio
but lost all the same,
drifting on a strange slumber.

GAY MEN DO NOT DIE ANYMORE

We say gay men do not die anymore—
just swallow down a cocktail, one small pill—
they search the bars for something to live for.

They wash up on this San Francisco shore
believing youth is immortality.
We say gay men do not die anymore.

Young, drunk demigods crossing the dancefloor,
free from any thoughts of those death mask days
they search the bars for something to live for.

Castro bartenders have a heavy pour,
so we drink for all those no longer here.
We say gay men do not die anymore.

I worry when they stumble out the door
because I know they won't be going home,
they search the bars for something to live for.

One night they will learn this is all folklore.
We age—still dying every day for love.
We say gay men do not die anymore.
They search the bars for something to live for.

TWELVE NOON BELLS

The bells of Holy Redeemer peel away
the morning fog. I am a fragile body,
whiskey-lodged, a tongue holding on
to the memory of last night's Manhattans,
nicotine on the lips.

The sun draws back the curtains,
the day of the Lord spilling across
the bedroom floor.   I cannot remember
the bars I haunted or how I returned
home, took off my clothes, tucked
myself in. And I cannot remember

the last time I dressed all Sunday best,
a white-pressed dress shirt, rosary
in the breast pocket, fingertips
dipped in holy water for the sign
of the cross.   God,

I said this wouldn't happen again.
Another day wasted piecing together
fragments, gazing through the prism
of a shot glass—crumbled dollar bills,
toppled tables, skinned knees stumbling
down Market Street. What am I chasing

when night is retreating and I am far
from stopping? Is it a religious ecstasy,
the spear of a seraphim?   I must quit this
like renouncing the church—a schism,
a censure on the dogma of youth,
the sacrament of self-doubt I
took on my tongue.   But

once Catholic, always Catholic.
It is baptized in my bones and I cannot

just unring the years, the habits of the past.
With the sheets twisted at my ankles
I can still recite it all—

May the Lord be with you.
       And also with you.
We lift up our hearts.
       We lift them up to the Lord.

I can see the body of Christ,
hoisted heavenward. I can hear the sharp
crack of communion bread. *Peace*
       I leave you, my peace I give you.

Lord I am not worthy to receive you,
but only say the word and I shall be healed.

The organ reverberates, "Holy God, We Praise
Thy Name," ushers God's children out the
church doors.   *Go in peace*
       to love and serve the Lord.

And I can still see all the young girls,
lace dresses, black patent shoes.   Life
is still simple, an easy mystery. They are gentle
as they remove their veils, strawberry blond hair
shining in the afternoon light. I pull the covers
over my head, and turn back to sleep.

ST. CHRISTOPHER

As a boy I was sure that death would find me
as I slept. Death like a dark shadow creeping
from the depths of the closet to the foot of the bed.

How could I not stumble into this fear? The Bible
filled with monsters and end days, seven devils,
a demon named Legion: *For we are many.*

So I wore your holy medal each and every night
as a Catholic talisman, a Third Century force,
as a garland of garlic to keep the vampires away.

I still see you—staff in hand, knee-deep in water.
I see the child Jesus perched on your shoulder,
his head a corona of light, the world in his tiny palm.

You carried him safely to the other shore—
patron saint of travelers, drowning boys
trying to cross over to adolescence.

When thunder rolled across the Ohio skies
and lightning cracked a whip across the ceiling,
I reached in for you, my hand in my shirt.

Your body pinched between finger and thumb
I prayed: *Watch over me, watch over,*
until I drifted into morning sun.

I still keep you safe in a cedar box
even when the church does not know
what do to with your feast day.

Removed from the Roman calendar,
the Vatican cannot verify your identity,
your story a mystic miscalculation.

The great canon of saints a revolving door,
a reshuffling of the deck—the newly beatified
brought to the fold, the old martyrs discarded.

St. Nicholas and the cult of Ursula,
St. George slaying the dragon, and you—
Christopher—fighting the river-wide tides.

When rain pounded the window panes,
who was I whispering to if not you?
Did anyone listen and ever answer back?

Or was I meant to learn
that I can hold the darkness alone
when heaven hides the stars away?

STARS

In San Francisco
you cannot see the stars—the planets
wrap themselves in night fog. So I go
searching for other forms of light.

The marquee of the Castro Theater
an exclamation point punctuating the sky.
And the people passing by shimmer and shine—
queens in their rhinestone gowns,
footfall lightning and thunder
in a size 12 pump.

I am a lost sailor
and they are the Seven Sisters,
the Pleiades descending from the darkness,
a chandelier earring sparkling in lamp glow.

They captain their own ship
and I follow their navigation to the Midnight Sun,
The Moby Dick Bar, where they obtain
a gravitational pull. The room shifts
as the eyes turn to gaze on this mythology,
this astronomical event in a thigh-high boot,
wigs teased to reach the troposphere.

No one can resist this orbit—
men become satellites leaning in
to light a cigarette, to carry their bags,
because we are all small creatures
seeking a fraction of this light,
this duality in fishnets,
a blood red lip.

Even I cannot escape the magnetic drag
that lures me across the bar to ask,
May I buy you a drink?

Vodka, a splash of cranberry.
It is an offering to the heavens,
to Libra—the great scales in perfect balance,
the male, the female
churning away within us all.

It is an offering to the day
when I too will glow—a nebula,
a cloud of dust moving along the sidewalk—
unashamed. But tonight I gaze
on the disco ball, its brilliant luminescence
spinning on the surface of my martini—
Andromeda floating on gin and vermouth.

THE GOD OF SAN FRANCISCO

Some believe the God of San Francisco
has taken his throne
at the top of Twin Peaks—
a mighty Mount Olympus
nine hundred feet above the city
where the kingdom of heaven
embraces the kingdom of The Bay.

At that elevation it is difficult not to see
that something greater guides the way,
watches over all creatures and creation
coming and going
by bridge and by air,
by cable car and ferry.

Watch as the west erupts with light,
the sun that drops into the Pacific
burning brighter than an angel
entering the atmosphere.
Watch the fog that follows,
floats like the Holy Ghost
down the rocky hillsides
to hang over Hayes Valley,
the Haight-Ashbury—
the sweetest incense
of some Catholic mass.

Yes, it is difficult not to believe,
but they are correct in name
and name alone—
my savior has a bar stool
at the Twin Peaks Tavern,
a window seat to watch the world
where Market Street meets Castro

and the rainbow flags flap in the cold
of another West Coast wind.

I go there when I need religion
at a happy hour price—
a Bud Light baptism—
when I need a good lesson
that God has yet to leave us behind.

He sits alone,
his hands turned to vein and bone.
But buy him a martini—
vodka with two olives,
extra dirty—
and he will tell you anything
you need to know,
from the Gold Rush to North Beach
where the sailors wore dresses
over their anchor tattoos,
to José Sarria and the Black Cat,
the Nightingale of Montgomery Street.

Yes, those were the days
when the prophets wore pearls,
when the Bible was burlesque,
and the saints mingled with the sinners,
the night a lightning strike
of arias and police sirens—
God Save Us Nelly Queens.

He raises a glass to the nevermore—
the 21st Street Baths,
the Elephant Walk,
to Harvey and his bullhorn.
A drink to the things that slipped away,
the bullets that shattered brains,
the murder called manslaughter

ushering in those White Night Riots,
the shattered glass of City Hall,
cop cars turned to funeral pyres.

And he remembers death
coming like it did in Egypt,
stealing the first born,
the second born,
any young man who fell in love
with the twilight over Polk Street.
The obituary pages
doubling every day
with the black and white faces
of the men who colored the Castro.

He can tell you how he washed the feet
of skinny boys with lesions,
boys in hospice beds
wheeled to the window
for one final look of the city at dawn,
then wheeled to the morgues
with no family to claim their remains.

So he took them—
all of them—
ashes upon ashes
collected and released
where the ocean waters worship
the glory of the Golden Gate.
He scattered them
in South of Market bars
where the men in leather tap a keg,
toast the life of another dead brother.

And he set them free
where the winds bow and bend,
genuflect for the San Francisco sky.

All the bodies that danced
in Folsom neon and Freedom Day parades,
in disco light and speakeasy darkness,
in the soft ballet of love and life,
they flutter and float forever
where the oceans wear
a halo from the moon,
and the towers of Twin Peaks
glow in the resurrection of the night.

GHOSTS IN LEATHER

I've seen ghosts
black and shiny—
a raven gliding
on the backdrop of midnight.

Boots spit cleaned,
jackets studded,
they take shape
the way smoke does
rising from an ashtray.

I've watched them
watching the living
in arthouse bathrooms,
bathhouse mazes.

I've seen them
the way I see you—
a motorcycle gang of angels,
bandana in the back pocket,
finger hooked through a belt loop.

It shouldn't be possible—
the dead are meant to wander in petticoats
in crumbling Victorians waiting
for 1906 to rock the foundations again.

They shiver in the fog
that floats above Fort Point,
muskets at the ready,
cannon fire rumbling on The Bay.

They certainly shouldn't be hovering
in the head rush of video cleaner,
in the heat and heart race
of the men's-only fitness club,

drifting like divine steam
from sauna to shower and back again.

And yet here they are,
phantasm voyeurs
puffing on cigars
in the glow of some VHS fantasy,
in the scratchy film and flesh
of dad teaching his boy a lesson.
Here they are like 1985
never died and faded away.

Perhaps heaven has no dungeons,
no black label on draft,
no hanky code or nod of the head
that says, *Follow me,*
my door is unlocked.

Perhaps these earthly places grab hold,
dominate the slanted pieces of our soul.
All this *yes sir,*
all this horse play and *good dog*
yanks a leash that tethers
the next life to this life.

All this beard on beard,
denim rubbing denim,
it lights a cigarette,
scatters sparks,
throws open a fire door
from the great eternal
to the back room of a dive bar,
to beer-soaked floors,
the tattooed arms of boys,
the salty taste of night's skin,
the tequila and tobacco tongue.

When we release spirit from body,
this is what I want—

to stumble back,
a drunk celestial being
knocking into the universe,
walking through whiskey walls
to a mirror ball limbo.

A shadow of a shadow
swaying along the sidewalks,
cruising the taverns and pubs
for those masters of mixology,
for those slaves of the physical world,
for the bartender who knows my order,
where my tab is always and forever open.

COFFIN WINDOWS

*Last month, a construction crew unearthed a small cast-iron coffin in a neighborhood
here that once housed a cemetery. Thousands of the city's dead were removed in
the early 1900s when politicians and developers pushed for more housing.*
— New York Times

Tiny coffin of bronze and lead,
two windows for peering in or
looking out. And here she is—
incorrupt. The casket air tight
so nothing could touch her
or steal her youth away. Forever
three years old when the construction
workers find her buried below
a concrete slab in the garage.

This neighborhood was a graveyard,
this city a cemetery. And it has been a century
since San Francisco cleared the dead.
Hundreds of thousands of bodies exhumed
to make way for the living,
for their bars and saloons, for tunnels
and trains and buildings
to block the sun.

So when the earth is moved again
we find her forgotten—left behind—
indigo flowers in her blond locks,
ivory christening dress and baby's breath.
If she was ever alone and scared
it is difficult to tell as she slumbers
like an iris waiting for spring.

The things she must have seen—
her family plucked from the ground,
the harvest of tombstones.
And what she must have felt
when the San Andres ripped apart,

her ankle boots kicking the coffin lid.
City Hall, the Palace Hotel, 500 city blocks
extinguished like a match.
Was she frightened when the fires
burned and raged for three days?

      No, she knew it was only death
coming to do what it does. Entombing
the past, enshrining the years gone by.
She held that cold hand long before
the living arrived to plant their new roots.
Brave child wandering ahead of us
to explore the unknown. Little pilgrim.
Immigrant to darkness, pioneer free of fear.
Stem of purple nightshade in her palm.

EARTHBOUND

I am told there are no sidewalks
where heaven is concerned.

No tic-tac-toe grids in the font
of a child's chalky hand. No

elms and pines and telephone polls
linking arms, guarding brick homes.

No factories, farms or forts
where men died in sweat and blood,

no line presses or tractors to witness
the soul's climb from the flesh. So

there is no need for mortuaries,
their rose garden wallpaper, flowers

and formaldehyde mingling,
conversing like old friends.

Headstone or cremation—
the decision is never made.

Perfect words a thing of the past.
Eulogies eulogized.

Mile after mile of pristine land
never soiled with a footprint,

land where no one kicked a stone
and shifted the semblance of space,

where no one built a barn,
turned dirt to stalks of corn,

where the air never tasted tobacco,
chimney smoke and gunpowder.

No locomotives shoved their way west,
robbing rusted towns of people. No one

left a family tree to splinter off,
left their history and fell apart.

So when I leave this body
I will stay right here

and watch the deer
eat roses from my grave,

watch concrete angels pray
for the world to begin again.

LANDS END, HALLOWEEN

Barely a soul wanders Lands End. The sun disappears
like everything that disappeared before—
The first Cliff House, Victorian chateau,
Gingerbread Palace burnt to cinders and black sand.
The Sutro Baths left for ruins. No more slides. No more
bathing caps and trapeze. Only ocean waves crashing
into concrete pools. And the Playland on the beach—
The Alpine Racer, the mirror maze, the carousel and
its Wurlitzer an echo on salty air.
        Everything vanishes—
even the last day of October surrenders to the grey
fog encroaching on the coast. It creeps up,
swallowing the crags of Seal Rock, pieces of sky and fading light,
the gull's skyward climb.   It hungers like a sea monster
and today is the day for indulging dark imagination.
So I drift into the fog to see what hides inside.
        The tentacles of the Kraken, cracking boats
in two. The Devil Whale sleeping like an island,
waiting to ambush, to open its jaws and devour
the ship and her crew. I see the Carolina Amelia
wrecked on Mile Rock, but sailing from the grave.
Ghost of a galleon. Queen Anne's Revenge. Pirates
rotting to bone but plundering the seas. And dead mariners,
drowned sailors, water-logged souls clustering together—lost
and confused. Feel their seaweed-slick fingertips touching
this world while the veil is still thin. Feel them reaching out
to drag the living down. Down to the ocean floor. The vast
depths of death. The cemeteries of the sea.
        But it is none of these. It is the day dying, night reborn.
It is the looming thunder clouds of time. The first of November
casting shadows on the shore.

THE BIRDS OF BODEGA BAY

What a way to go—
to release the soul to the sound
of seagulls screaming, wings beating
on a fur coat, glass breaking
in a phone booth.

Death, that's when you were a leading man,
dressed as your mother, ripping back
the shower curtain, slashing again and again
the delicate 35-millimeter skin.   *Mother,*
oh God Mother, blood
blood.

You were a matinee idol,
strangling your rival with a rope,
stashing him in a wooden chest,
then inviting the party guests.
The chest set for a buffet
and no one the wiser. Yes,
you were a Hollywood star,
a glowing Manhattan skyline.

But these days you have lost your panache,
your big screen appeal.
You take the role of the wheelchair,
breathing machine,
a virus wandering through the bloodstream.

Try to remember
when you were box office gold.
Remember the tombs of Mission Dolores,
the mysterious lady in gray,
her graceful fall into the San Francisco Bay.
Remember the nun walking out of darkness
and the great plunge from the bell tower
of San Juan Bautista.

I want to know you
as the red carpet talk of the town,
a fresh new starlet on your arm,
not the cancer ward in Beverly Hills,
the sleepless night in Malibu
waking to cool air and wet sheets,
dementia and confusion
unable to remember the golden age
of the marquee.

So when you come for my curtain call,
spare me the hospital bed, the hospice.
Come to me as a pair of love birds
spurring on the end times.
Come as a playground covered with crows.
Come as a sky of talons
descending on Bodega Bay.

GREYHOUND

When I close my eyes
and leave this world behind
let me open them again

as a greyhound waking,
stretching out my lean limbs
to yawn and greet the foggy day.

Unleashed, unmuzzled,
I trot alongside you
in this city of Saint Francis

where all animals are blessed
but dogs are familiars, demigods,
free to roam the streets like royalty.

Let me be your four-legged
reincarnation, recklessly chasing
the shadow of my tail. Let me be

your spring-stepped Jack Russell
running amok in Dolores Park, kicking up
dirt, licking sunshine from the pavement.

Let me be your golden retriever
rushing towards the Golden Gate Bridge
on the sandy shores of Baker Beach

where the men slip off their speedos
to sun their muscled asses and feel
the soft fingers of the ocean air.

I'll be your wingman at the bar—
a black lab beating my tail on the barstool,
pacing the beer-soaked floors for boys

who will scream, *What a cutie,*
and kiss me on the nose. With any luck
he'll kiss you too. A perfect team—

your good boy, your dance partner,
your Great Dane with paws on your shoulders
swaying to the music on the radio.

Your playmate, your fashion plate,
your French bulldog in spiked collar and beret,
lazy and bellyful from biscuits and love.

This could be our every day—you and me
going everywhere, teacup chihuahua
stowing away in the pocket of your coat.

The museum or a matinee—
two admissions for the price of one,
me nibbling popcorn from your palm.

I'll race you down the Embarcadero,
a long-haired dachshund or basset hound,
floppy ears bouncing off the sidewalk.

Your spirit guide, your protector,
I'll bark at the sea lions on Pier 39,
chase the seagulls from Fisherman's Wharf.

Your purebreed or your loyal mutt,
it doesn't matter much when the sun
sets on Washington Square

and your fingertips roam across my belly,
when you scratch that place behind my ear
and my legs shake like I'm running on air.

Spotted beagle or some poodle mix,
it makes no difference at all
when the evening chill makes landfall

and we journey home through darkness
to stars in the windows,
to soft pillows and heavy blankets.

Let me snore in the crook of your arm,
my cold nose on your warm skin,
dreaming of the next day set to begin.

DRAGONFLY

As a girl in Vera Cruz
your mother captured dragonflies—
snatched them from the warm air—
careful not to damage their translucent wings.
Vibrating in her hand
she tied a neat knot to the thorax.
And once secure she let them go,
released them to soar
but never soar away.
A little insect as kite
made to fly but stay,
fluttering along in the orange glow
of a Mexican sun.

I believe you have done the same for me.
A fragile body in your palm—voluntary—
asking for a gentle tether.
I do not need it but love it
when I feel the tug of your wires,
when I fly over Alcatraz, the Golden Gate,
when my feet graze the rooftop of the Ferry Building.
You guide my flight
even when I wander back east
over a time zone or two.
You hold me secure,
my life entwined around your fingertips.

MY DEPARTURE

I refuse to believe it is all dreamless sleep,
a blanket of night covering the memories of life.

But no one has returned from that strange valley
and Lazarus never explained where he went.

So we must leave something behind—
a tether that ties two planes together.

Perhaps it will be these simple lines
or silent times when words were not needed,

evening starlight shining through the window,
my arms wrapped around you until morning.

And then the lazy day unwinding before us—
aroma of coffee, crow cackling in the trees,

two dogs softly nestled between us
under an afghan my grandmother crocheted.

And finally when we rise the afternoon awaits,
sun in the trees, lilac and lavender,

wisteria petals pinwheeling on open wind—
the Sunday sky like cathedral glass.

Pluck these things from the air,
press them into the pages of a book

like a martyr's cloth, the bone of a saint,
a miraculous medal that binds our worlds.

And when you reach back for these things
perhaps they will pull back at me.

It yanks a great chain of electricity,
violently tugs on fetters of lightning.

For one moment we are shocked to life again,
the darkness of the heavens dismantled.

Our eyes wide and blinded
by brilliant blue mornings we knew.

JESUS DESCENDS ON GOLDEN GATE PARK

The children have chased down their final pastel eggs.
And the church bells have exhausted their Hallelujahs,
    He has risen.
        He has risen indeed.
Now the park is overflowing with men showing off
their Easter bonnets—Cadbury cream concoctions
of hot glue and plastic flowers.

Now come the Sisters of Perpetual Indulgence—saints
of the night celebrating the holiest of days, the life everlasting. So
their winged habits point to eternity. And their arms are outstretched
to bless the crowds of heathens, the beautiful blasphemers.

We are all waiting for the savior to rise again. We are all waiting
for the Hunky Jesus Contest to begin.

    One Jesus after another takes the stage
like the son of man standing before Pilot. But
no one calls for crucifixion, only a passion play,
a cast of Christs stripped to a loin cloth, a jock strap,
crowns of thorns and lipstick stigmata.

They are all here—the carpenter's son
with his tool belt and CrossFit abs. Christ in a harness,
leather chaps, nipple rings like little haloes.
    Jesus in bunny ears.
        Jesus in lingerie.
            Jesus in fishnets
crossdressing his way through Nazareth.

This is a Catholic school expulsion, a Vatican heresy,
and yet we have just begun.
    In comes Christ on roller skates.
        A cheerleading Christ, shaking pompoms, doing the splits.
          Rock star Jesus with a crucifix guitar. Suddenly,

clouds of smoke rise and the Christ of Haight-Ashbury appears—
bare-footed, dreadlocked, water bubbling in a glass bong.

The Midwest grandmas clutch their rosaries.
The Pentecostal bishops hold their bibles high.
And the Televangelists speak in tongues—
      we are the spit in God's eye,
          we are the Sodom and Gomorrah of the West. And soon
we will turn to pillars of salt. Soon we will pay a heavy price.
Earth cracking open. Bay turned to blood. Frogs raining from the sky.
And disease and plague and darkness for three days.

      No one knows darkness like the men and women standing
shoulder to shoulder in Golden Gate Park celebrating
resurrection.

      These San Francisco elders. This Castro royalty.
This order of nuns in corsets and leather. They were here for darkness
when others ran the other way.   Do not preach to them of plague.
Extinction. That Old Testament God flooding the world
to start over again.

More dead than a century of Sundays.
Calvary Hill in a hospice bed. A decade of church doors
locked tight.   Priests sleeping through the 80s.
      Ministers of God's wrath condemning the 90s.

So who anointed the sick?
      Who were the disciples guiding soul from body?
         Who buried the children of God?
Who shined the love of Christ into the shadows of mortality?

It was the queens and queers. The altar boy runaways
and Catholic school refugees. The dying caring for the dying.
Adopted brothers and sisters descending into hell
     again and again,
         day after day,

until light somehow found a way in.

So this day of the Lord, this end of Lent,
is all for them. The old God of vengeance is dead.
The Christ of compassion,
         the Christ of understanding,
                  the Christ of love is here today
reborn again in Golden Gate Park.

NORTH BEACH

The mist turns to rain over Columbus Avenue and I am reminded
    of all the things I will never be. This neighborhood built
    by Italian hands. A good Catholic man. The Church of Saints
    Peter and Paul. These streets named for poets. Jack Kerouac.
    Bob Kaufman. The great temple of Ferlinghetti.

It's been years since I stepped inside a holy place, took to my knees,
    confessed my shortcomings. And far too long since I opened
    the throat of a poem and made it sing. So I search for the muses
    in Washington Square. I commune with the dead in Caffé Trieste.
    I lasso the ghosts that rise when the cathedral bells chime. And I
    hold them until they dissolve as ocean foam slipping through my hands.

There are poems wandering around in my head, lost somewhere near
    Lombard and Stockton. They trail away to watch the parrots
    glide off for Coit Tower. Sometimes they walk out into the bay,
    content to marry the waves, uninterested in allowing me to write
    them down. It is then I am sure I will never write anything great.

It is then I am sure I will never dine at the Last Supper sharing wine
    with the apostles. I will never find myself in the canon of saints,
    the great canon of poets, the ancient lineage that breathes life
    into the next life. My lines will never sigh like the psalms of
    King David. And my voice will never sound like Whitman
    whispering to Ginsberg—Howl.

My words will never save the great minds of my generation, walking
    aimless, adrift in San Francisco, searching for the grand meaning
    of it all. Searching for a poem taller than the Transamerica, built
    tight to float on the Pacific, touched by God to make disciples
    weep.

I may never find it. But here we are—where the Beats ran through the
    streets, screaming into the night. Here we are under the same sky
    where the poets raised a glass to the moon, raged at the words
    that would not come. Here we are where the poets loved, lived,
    dreamt, died.

Tonight the darkness over North Beach burns brighter than Point Bonita.
The traffic turns puddles of rain into halos. The lanterns in
Chinatown flicker in the distance. The windows of City Lights
shine with a warm glow. Shadows move in the poetry room.
And I am awash in a sudden fire. I am blessed just to be here.

ST. ANNE

The priest said,
God is in your typewriter.
So you went there
with your star rats,
with your awful rowing.

The clacking of keys
could wake Christ from the cross.
Letters striking the page,
a communion with the dead,
a confessional
to burn down the Earth of Genesis
and rebuild from ash
a sonnet, a prayer,
a spirit healed from sickness.

Perhaps it made you weary,
all this birth and rebirth,
all this creation
with no Sabbath for rest.
And all the sadness
blooming again like spring.

So you poured the vodka,
pulled on your mother's fur coat,
locked the garage, turned over the engine—
martyred by carbon monoxide
to sleep,
to float away.

I wonder if any of it saved you,
all the Bedlam and folly,
all the words bleeding through inked ribbon.
I believe I find the answer
when I reach for your stanzas
and they reach back,

touching the great unknown.
It trembles inside me,
shifts and returns again,
and I consider you canonized.

IBLIS

On cold, unforgiving mornings I think of God,
how the echo of an empty tomb is like God.

This is when Iblis accepts my invitation,
crosses the desert, warms my hands like a fire god.

We pour the whiskey on the cemetery lawn,
discuss creation, the decisions made by God.

Heaven and Earth born as one then ripped asunder—
mountains, rocks taking shape as commanded by God.

And from the dirt, sand, and water Adam was birthed,
his eyes suddenly alive with the breath of God.

All the angels and all the jinn ordered to bow
before ordinary man formed from clay by God.

But Iblis is eternal, forged from smokeless fire,
and some demands are demeaning, even from God.

It was the first rebellion, the first cosmic war,
the first creature of free will to say no to God.

And so it goes Iblis was cast from the gardens,
left to roam Earth's catacombs by a petty God.

He's a child who must have his own way, says Iblis,
as he pours another glass, raises it to God.

Some would say Iblis is nothing but Prince of Lies,
but I have seen what happens when men act like God—

A child kneeling to a darkness dressed in vestments,
churches turned to charnel houses larger than God,

the bones of victims stacked in filing cabinets,
all the once faithful freezing from their loss of God.

I watch ice melt from the graves and Iblis whispers,
James, build your fire without the help of man or God.

IN THE HAMMAM WE ARE CALLED TO PRAYER

Naked except for the checkered peshtemal
loose at my waist. I wait for the young man
who will clean the dirty streets from my torso,
wash away the long day exploring the avenues
of Istanbul.

     I wait
as the heat hugs the ancient marble and
the call to prayer breaks the evening silence,
rattles the steam-slicked walls.

    Allah is the greatest   *Allah is the greatest*
    Allah is the greatest   *Allah is the greatest*

Soon I hear the wet patter of sandaled feet
echoing in the damp vestibule. It is a rhythm,
a percussion, a nasheed to shake the tiled floors.
It enters my chest, rattles my bones.

Bare-chested, wrapped in a cloth that matches mine,
he orders me to lift my arms. Lathers my pits
with a mitted cloth. He explores my chest and stomach,
moves down to reach the middle of my back.

    There is no God but God No God but God

He directs my body. Tells me what to do.
Back flat on the stone he soaps my chest,
suds my legs, the bottom of my feet. Then
comes the buckets of warm water, a spiritual
cascade drenching my limbs. Next

he lies me face down, removes my towel,
exposes me discreetly and never fully. He covers
my backside and continues scrubbing
shoulders, spine, nape of neck, inner thighs.

I bear witness that Muhammad is the messenger of God
I bear witness that Muhammad is the messenger of God

I could fall in love with this ritual,
this sacrament of sultans and common men.
I could fall in love with these Kurdish hands,
the sweat of his skin anointing my flesh,
the breath of his lungs dancing a dervish
the length of crown to toe. But

this is not sensual. No sexuality in this centuries
of service. Men cleansing the bodies of men.
For the law is clear: *You came in lust to men*
in preference to women. No, you are indeed a people
transgressing beyond bounds.

So I keep my hands at my side and consider the line—
in desert towns and cities on the sea the men
walk hand in hand, arm in arm. It is kinship.
Brotherhood and solidarity.

In the Saudi villages and Pakistan streets
they greet one another with lips to cheeks.
And in the Turkish baths along the Bosphorus
the men discard their clothes, give themselves
over to baptism.

Hasten to prayer Hasten to Prayer

His eyes meet mine and I burn.
Catholic boy. Ohio born and blessed
by Islamic fingers. His body as bare as mine
I offer up a supplication as the minarets quake.

This thunder is beautiful. Terrifying.
It is a shower of fire. Brimstone.
Biblical cities destroyed.
A Sodom and Gomorrah crumbling again.

Hasten to success Hasten to Success

In the barren cities of theocracy
this thought, this action, this love
is a town square noose. A stone to the head.
A fall from the tower. Body smashed on cobbles.

I have rinsed away the remains of those religions,
the book of Leviticus, the dogma I was steeped in.
I wonder if he has done the same. Closed the Qur'an.
Purified the message of angels.

God is the greatest   God is the greatest

I wonder if he has washed away the blood
of swords, verses of violence, embraces the teaching:
*Hold to forgiveness, command what is right,
and turn away from the ignorant.*

He turns me around, dries my hair,
wraps me in clean linens and offers me
water, tea, a cigarette. I pay him his lira
and return to the dark streets.
A crescent moon overhead.

There is no deity but God No deity but God

REVELATION

Ohio southbound
the radio band cracks.
Two frequencies fight in the airwaves.
The day's top hits fade to static
as the Gospel scratches and pops.

We are entering the Kingdom of the Lord.
Blood orange sun.
Moon like a crowned dragon
sliding into view.
Farmhouses and chapels,
a clapboard barn proclaiming
Jesus Saves.

The end times are speeding this way.
Twilight lurking on the horizon,
the Anti-Christ waiting to be born.
The Apocalypse of John
ricocheting through the atmosphere.

In the interstate silence,
darkness closing in,
it is hard not to fear
a great beast of the sea,
feet like a bear, mouth like a lion,
rising over the land,
looming over the transmission towers—
six-armed monsters marching into war.

It is hard not to marvel
at the planets and satellites
shifting in space,
the wormwood star—
a torch of destruction—
tumbling toward Earth.

The minister's voice hisses
from the speaker. He urges,
he implores: *There is still time to repent.*
Still time to change direction.

But no one is listening.
No truckers or tankers,
gas station idolaters.
No unbelievers.
Only the never-ending acres
and the horses—
black, white, and pale—
their muzzles misting the cold air.

Tonight I am the only soul
and this road continues forever.
Each highway exit a reincarnation,
a resurrection of the dead.
And the seven angels sounding their trumpets
are train whistles shattering the night.

NO OBITS

We tried not to get too excited about it too soon ...
So we waited patiently, quietly, to see how many this week's mail would bring.
And then there were none ...
— Bay Area Reporter, *August 1998*

Summer in San Francisco is never this warm, yet
here we are. Ninety degrees in August. The hottest day
of the year.
     The flowers have dragged their blooms from the basement.
The fog packed away for another day. And this season's crop of young men
have shed their clothes on the lawns of Dolores Park. Their pale, bony
torsos have turned to copper. Turned to mercury.
     They are becoming something more. And now we see
that anything is possible.

     Even today's news is possible. The front page fluttering
on a park bench—*No obits*—as though death has quit his job,
taken a much-deserved rest.
     For years the names poured in. A deluge.
The editor's inbox flooded with crisp white envelopes,
handwritten return addresses staring back like an epitaph. Piles
of human history type-spaced on an ancient typewriter. A life
folded neatly—a shroud—holding a photo, the face of someone now gone,
journeying off to the dark mystery we all fear.

     Now the bay breeze flips the front page to the classifieds,
the arts section, an ad for the opera, the Tea Room Theater. And the past
comes back as a whisper—we were a generation betrayed
by government. The face of Reagan. Betrayed by a silence that shouted:
     There is nothing to see here.
     There is nothing that can be done.

Our families buried us before we could die.
And the family we adopted lived as they stood dying, refusing
the betrayal of our own bodies. An inside job. Our cells
resisting the cocktail of pills. Thrush and sarcoma.

And still we sipped sidecars with the North Beach crowds—
the Beat boys at Vesuvio, the queens of Finnochio's on Broadway—
because this life was worth hanging on to. Our halos
cabaret lights burning until burning out.

Next week, perhaps next month, when September
rolls off the ocean, the season will cool. The chill
of mortality settling in the air.
But today the city is a warm hand. A lost friend
inviting us to stretch our limbs on the green grass. To feel
the sun's rays on our skin. One day this will blink out.
Fade away. Die. But not yet.
Not today.

ACKNOWLEDGMENTS

The following poems in this collection first appeared in the following journals and publications.

"Autumn Burning" / *COG*

"Bilingual" / *The Fourth River*

"Earthbound" / *Flights*

"Falling Asleep To The Sound Of Fog Horns I Dream Of Ohio" / *COG*

"Gay Cancer" / *Codex Journal*

"The God Of San Francisco" / *HIV Here & Now*

"Ghosts In Leather" / *The Good Men Project*

"In The Hammam We Are Called To Prayer" / *Foglifter*

ABOUT THE POET

James J. Siegel is a San Francisco-based poet and literary arts organizer. He is the host and curator of the popular monthly Literary Speakeasy show at Martuni's piano bar. Originally from Toledo, Ohio, his first poetry collection, *How Ghosts Travel*, was inspired and fueled by his coming of age in the Midwest and was a finalist for an Ohioana Book Award. He was a scholarship recipient to the Antioch Writers' Workshop in Yellow Springs, Ohio, and his poems have been featured in a number of journals including *The Cortland Review, Borderlands: Texas Poetry Review, Assaracus, The Fourth River, HIV Here & Now, The Good Men Project*, and more. He was also featured in the anthology *Divining Divas: 100 Gay Men On Their Muses*.

ABOUT THE PRESS

Sibling Rivalry Press is an independent press based in Little Rock, Arkansas. It is a sponsored project of Fractured Atlas, a nonprofit arts service organization. Contributions to support the operations of Sibling Rivalry Press are tax-deductible to the extent permitted by law, and your donations will directly assist in the publication of work that disturbs and enraptures. To contribute to the publication of more books like this one, please visit our website and click *donate*.

Sibling Rivalry Press gratefully acknowledges the following donors, without whom this book would not be possible:

Anonymous (18)

Arkansas Arts Council

John Bateman

W. Stephen Breedlove

Dustin Brookshire

Sarah Browning

Billy Butler

Asher Carter

Don Cellini

Nicole Connolly

Jim Cory

Risa Denenberg

John Gaudin

In Memory of Karen Hayes

Gustavo Hernandez

Amy Holman

Jessica Jacobs & Nickole Brown

Paige James

Nahal Suzanne Jamir

Allison Joseph

Collin Kelley

Trevor Ketner

Andrea Lawlor

Anthony Lioi

Ed Madden & Bert Easter

Mitchell, Blackstock, Ivers & Sneddon, PLLC

Stephen Mitchell

National Endowment for the Arts

Stacy Pendergrast

Simon Randall

Paul Romero

Randi M. Romo

Carol Rosenfeld

Joseph Ross

In Memory of Bill Rous

Matthew Siegel

Alana Smoot

Katherine Sullivan

Tony Taylor

Leslie Taylor

Hugh Tipping

Guy Traiber

Mark Ward

Robert Wright